THUNDERBOOM! POEMS FOR EVERYONE

thunderbOOm!

POEMS FOR EVERYONE

Charlotte Pomerantz

PICTURES BY

Rob Shepperson

FRONT STREET

Asheville, North Carolina

Library of Congress Cataloging-in-Publication Data
Pomerantz, Charlotte.
Thunderboom!: poems for everyone / Charlotte Pomerantz;
pictures by Rob Shepperson.— 1st ed.
p. cm.
ISBN 1-932425-40-3 (alk. paper)
1. Children's poetry, American.
I. Shepperson, Rob. II. Title.
PS3566.O538T48 2005
811'.54–dc22   2005012053

FRONT STREET
An Imprint of Boyds Mills Press, Inc.
A Highlights Company

For Sharon Burrell

THUNDERBOOM! POEMS FOR EVERYONE

CONTENTS

CONTENTS

Here They Come

Ladies and gentlemen,
Your attention, please:
The parade of animals is about to begin!

Tootle the fife,
Rattle the drum,
Blow on the doodlesack,
Here they come!

A chowder of cats?
A cloud of gnats?

Hey!
Who is throwing those clackety toys?
Who is making that yakkety noise?

A husk of hares?
A sloth of bears?
A brood of eels?
A plump of seals?
A walk of snails?
A pod of whales?
A watch of tiny
Nightingales?

Tootle-ootle that fife,
Rattle-attle that drum,
Doodle-oodle that sack,
'Cause here they come.

Thumping doodlesacks,
Look at them come!

It's a crush,
A rush,
A group,
A troop.

A cram,
A jam,
A crunch,
A bunch.

A huddle,
A muddle,
A kit and caboodle,
A pile,
A press,
A whole toot and toodle,
A hodgepodge,
A mess ...

That's who's making
That hullabaloo,
That rackety-clackety
Bing-bang noise—
It's a ragtag, boodlebag,
Ragamuffin crew
Of yak-yak-yakkety
Girls and boys!

Merry-Go-Round

The hooves of my mighty horse
thunder the ground.
"Hi, Grandpa. Hi, Grandpa,"
I wave, going round.
"Faster, go faster,"
I yell to my horse.
Who'll win the gold ring?
I will, of course.

The hooves of my mighty horse
no longer thunder.
The music is stopping …
is stopping,
is still.

Who won the gold ring,
I wonder, I wonder.
"Don't worry," says Grandpa,
"next time you will."

Would You Care to Share Your Pear?

"Would you care to share your pear
with me, the friendly Growly Bear?
I could sit upon your chair
and we could share that yummy pear."

*"Excuse me, good friend Growly Bear,
but don't I see you sitting there
upon a large and comfy chair
munching your own yummy pear?"*

"Yes, it's me, the Growly Bear,
but I want more than just one pear.
Don't you think it's only fair
that you share your yummy pear?"

*"What makes you think my yummy pear
is something that I care to share
with you, you greedy Growly Bear?"*

"Grr, grr, little grrrl—beware!
Beware the froshus Growly Bear.
If you do not share your pear,
I will walk from here to there,
push you off your comfy chair,
and eat you and your yummy pear!"

*"Poof, you greedy Growly Bear,
I'll take up your silly dare!"*

So she walked from here to there,
pushed the Growly off his chair,
and *gobbled up* his yummy pear.

"Mmmmmmm."

It was indeed
the nicest pear
that she had tasted anywhere.
And
MUCH,
MUCH,
MUCH too good to share!

Cat and Rat

Meow, said the cat,
pit-a-pat, what's that?

It is I, a rat,
running past you, cat.

What's your hurry, friend rat?
Do stop and chat.

No, no, friend cat.
I must run, pit-a-pat.
I'm a tasty rat.
You're a hungry cat.
Even words of friendship
cannot change that.

Bye-bye, friend cat,
Pit-a-pat pat pat.

Stem and Stone

Look at stem.
Look at stone.
Stem has a flower.
Stone is alone.
Stem bends a little.
Stone doesn't bend.
Stem blooms and dies.
Stone has no end.

Stone has no end.
Stem lives again.

Thunderboom!

The brightening
of lightning
is sudden, swift,
and strong.

The sound of
thunderboom
is fifty letters long:

        donder
        donner
        dunner
        raam

        torden
        tondro
        radi
        hrom

        raad
        GROM!

(Note: The words mean "thunder" in many languages.)

My Favorite Seasons

My favorite seasons of them all
are winter, summer, spring, and fall.
And every time those seasons come,
I love to beat my little drum.

Snow Upon Root

Snow upon root
Dove against sky
Under my window
Love passes by.

No snow upon root
No dove against sky
Under my window
Love has passed by.

The snow will return
As will the dove
And since hope lives forever
So will my love.

Boots

I like the crunch of boots,
Mine and those beside me
And those in back
That make a track
And those in front
That guide me.

Bloomsday

A lady called Molly—yes!—Bloom
Kept Leopold plants in her room.
When friends cried, "Enough!"
She replied in the buff,
"Let a thousand Leopolds Bloom."

For Carlo

From sparrow peep to evenglow,
You're with me everywhere I go.
From evenglow to sparrow peep,
You're in the pocket of my sleep.

Drowsy Bees

The drowsy bumbling bumblebee
And the humming humblebee
Are, as you will plainly see,
The selfsame busy buzzy bee.

For the bumbling bumblebee
Is always humming drowsily,
While the humming humblebee
Bumbles oh so bumbily.

Therefore, since the bumble hums,
He is called a humblebee;
Likewise, since the humble bums,
He is called a bumblebee.

Unless, of course, these be *shee*-bees;
Wherefore, to put them at their ease,
You'd call them humble bumble shees,
Or humble drowsy bumble shees.

That way, you'd be sure to pleez z z z z z z z z z.

Presents for Everybody

Thick wool mittens for Johnny Begg.
For the Puzzle Lady, a scrambled egg.

For Roaring Peter and Frisky Shorty,
A fisherman's rod, left-handed and sporty.

For Treacle Tom and Sully the Thug,
A nice cup of tea in a porcelain mug.

A fork and knife for Uncle Fudge.
A slotted spoon for Puff-Puff Pudge.

For Andy McKenzie, slush mince pies.
For Isabella, adoring eyes.

Picture postcards for Lonesome Waggy.
A letter to last a lifetime for Maggie.

For the bully boys, Flap and Flip,
A seasick trip on a government ship.

For Lawdy Daw and Lady Don,
A plumped-up cushion to lie upon.

For Shem, a pen to write a tale.
For Shawn, a bag to carry the mail.

For Kitty Colrain of Butterman's Lane,
A pigeon stain on her window pane.

A prize every morning for Steadfast Dick.
For Stumblestone Davy, a walking stick.

For drowsy Megpeg Woppington,
A cart to get her shopping done.

For Agnus Daisy and Snakeshead Lil,
Nutmeg crushed in a magic pill.

A paper cup for Penceless Pete,
To pick up sunbeams from the street.

For Ida-Ida, goldeny bellows
To fan the fire and warm the fellows.

A place down here for the Man in the Moon.
For Selene up there, a starry balloon.

For Will-o'-the-Wisp and Barney-the-Bark,
Fair weather, so they can sleep in the park.

A horsehair bag for Grandma Fritz
In which to spit her cherry pits.

For Uncle Foozle and Auntie Jack,
A photo of me, if they ever come back.

MERRY CHRISTMAS!

The Know-It-All Cat

Said the first little cat
to the know-it-all cat,
"I took a trip
on a sailing ship."
  "Been there, done that,"
  said the know-it-all cat.

Said the second little cat
to the know-it-all cat,
"I climbed so high
I touched the sky."
  "Been there, done that,"
  said the know-it-all cat.

Said the third little cat
to the know-it-all cat,
"I looked at a cloud
and laughed out loud."
  "Been there, done that,"
  said the know-it-all cat.

Said the fourth little cat
to the know-it-all cat,
"I made a friend
around the bend."
  "Did *what*? How's *that*?"
  said the know-it-all cat.

"I made a friend
around the bend."

"Bless my whiskers!"
said the know-it-all cat.
"I've *never* been there
and I've *never* done that!"

Finn Again

Finn was out, but now he's in again.
He's in love and in a spin again.
You may laugh, but you won't grin again.

Chang was yang, but now he's yin again.
He bumped his nose and hit his chin again.
Rex was stout, but now he's thin again.

Must you play that violin again?
Bang on wood but not on tin again.
My trousers ripped! I'll need a pin again.

Writ this day by Mrs. Flanagan

The Moonstruck Witch

The witch on her broomstick sleeps half the day
And wakes in the late afternoon
To sweep out the light, then the dark, on her way
To race 'cross the face of the moon.

The old moon waits for the galloping flight
Of the witch of the night on her broom.
When he sees her ride by, he glows with delight.
When she passes, he sinks into gloom.

"If only she'd slow down her galloping pace,"
Thought the moon, "we could chat for a while.
For though I am old and have lines on my face,
I do have a luminous smile."

Thought the witch on her broomstick, "I dare not stop,
For I'm nothing but old bones and skin.
My hair is a twisted and tangly mop.
My nose nearly touches my chin."

"The old witch must know of my dark, hidden side,"
Thought the lonely and sorrowing moon.
"For though it's the side that at all times I hide,
One learns of it later or soon."

"Alas," cried the witch, in a moonstruck rage,
"I'm too ugly to show him the truth.
I dare not attempt a love spell at my age.
I shall put on the soft mask of youth."

That night, the witch wore a lovely young face
And dismounted her broom in the light.
"Ah me," breathed the moon, "you ride with such grace.
But where is the witch of the night?"

"She is dead," said the lovely young voice in disguise.
"I am her beautiful daughter.
The old witch was galloping 'cross the night skies
When she slipped and fell into the water."

The bewitched old moon groaned aloud and turned pale.
All that glowed were a few feeble beams.
"Oh, daughter, you come with a terrible tale,
For you speak of the witch of my dreams."

He sobbed like a child. "Oh, nobody knows
How I loved the old witch of the night.
As far back in time as my moon memory goes,
I rejoiced in her galloping flight."

The old witch ripped off her mask and cried,
"You forget, I am ugly and old."
But the pale moon peered out and tenderly sighed,
"Come to me, for I'm lonely and cold."

The old witch blinked hard to hold back the tears,
For the moon's eyes spoke nothing but truth.
She cast off her garment of deep-woven fears.
She tore up the false mask of youth.

She rode toward the waiting moon, and soon
The moon in his arms did enfold her.
And every night, the witch and the moon
And their love grow older and older.

The Courtship of Mole and Vole

A shy little mole
lived alone in a hole
and was lonesome by night and by day

'til a spry little vole
tumbled into the hole
and said, "Oh, how nice. May I stay?"

"Stay with me?" said the mole.
"That can't be," said the mole.
"No, no, no … maybe so … yes, okay."

"Thank you, mole," said the vole
as she unpacked a bowl
and put cups for tea on a tray.

"Tea for two," said the vole.
"Me and you?" said the mole.
"That sounds very nice, I must say."

"Yessiree," said the vole.
"Wait and see," said the vole.
"Do you take milk, by the way?"

"Milk in tea!" exclaimed mole,
almost losing control.
"The thought of it turns my hair gray."

"How 'bout sugar?" said vole.
"Yes, nine lumps," replied mole.
"Nine lumps!" cried the vole in dismay.

"In a mug," said the mole.
"Oh, ugh!" exclaimed vole.
"I don't think I could drink it that way."

"Mugs are cheery," said mole.
"Mugs are dreary," said vole.
"As sad as a lonely gray day."

"How can we have tea
if we cannot agree?" cried vole.
"Do try it my way!"

"Since you don't like a mug,"
said the mole with a shrug,
"I suppose ... a cup ... is okay."

Then the spry little vole
Kissed the shy little mole
And said, "You are smart, I must say."

Said the mole, "I'm not smart,
but I do have a heart,
and where there's a will there's a way."

"I love tea," said the vole.
"I love thee," said the mole.
"Let us whistle a sweet roundelay."

"I can't whistle," said vole.
"Then I'll whistle," said mole.
"Let us go and be married today!"

"Today?" said the vole.
"Yes, today," said the mole.
"Let me first put these teacups away."

Wedding Song of Mole and Vole

Something old
Something new
Something borrowed
And blue
In the lovely old way.

Love is old
Love is new
Borrowed evermore
For you
On this bright, blue-eyed day.

With these rings, we are wed.
Let us eat the fresh-baked bread
And sing again this merry roundelay
This very merry round-go-roundelay.

The Kangaroo

A kangaroo doesn't keep in her pocket
Bracelets or brooches or rings or a locket.

She doesn't keep pencils and lollipop sticks
Or bubblegum wrappers or magical tricks.

She doesn't keep cookies or cornsticks to munch
Or crispy salt crackers or celery to crunch.

She doesn't keep postcards or bent paper clips
Or yo-yos or tickets from trolleybus trips.

She doesn't keep thimbles or licorice drops
Or Cracker Jacks, whistles, or peppermint pops.

She keeps in her pocket—can you guess who?

A baby kangaroo.

Good Night, Margaret Wise Brown

In the great green room
There was a cellular phone
And a Mylar balloon
And a picture of
A Mars probe hurtling past the moon
And three endangered bears
On inflatable chairs
And Internet-bought socks
And digital clocks
And a virtual dollhouse
And an ergonomic mouse
And a bowl full of high-fiber low-carb mush
And a baby monitor murmuring "hush."
Good night, room
Good night, moon
Good night, Mars probe hurtling past the moon
Good night, stars
Good night, air
And random acoustics everywhere
Good night, city
Good night, town
Good night,
Margaret
Wise
Brown.

Shoes

Look what I found.
Shoes!

Shoes for biking
Shoes for hiking

Shoes for jumping
Shoes for bumping

Shoes with bows
And open toes

A shoe for you
A shoe for me
Fancy shoes for serving tea

Shoes to wiggle in
Shoes to giggle in
Shoes that you can wiggle
And giggle in

Shoes to be glad in
Shoes to be sad in
Monster shoes to be big
And bad in

So many different kinds of shoes—
How am I supposed to choose?

I know …

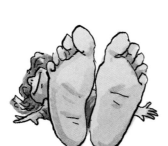

I'll line them up along the wall
And then I'll choose …

NO SHOES AT ALL!

Song of the Humpback Whale

O mighty and belovèd Yahweh,
Lord of earth and heaven,
You who made the dry lands
And the seas that number seven,
You who did divide the awesome darkness
From the light,
You who made the whale, the fish,
The wingèd bird in flight,
You who made all human life
And every creature living,
To You I owe my days, my dreams,
My song of deep thanksgiving.

Jonah's Song

Jonah: Here sit I in the belly of a fish,
By Yahweh quite forsaken.
Here sit I in the belly of a fish,
Wet and badly shaken.

Whale: I've dined on baby shrimp in brine
In all the seven seas,
But never has my humpback spine
Been jabbed by knobby knees.

Jonah: How alone I feel, how utterly alone,
In the watery land of the dead.

Whale (burping): Me? I'd gladly be alone
than feel so overfed.

Jonah: Here I sit in the belly of a fish,
Abandoned, lost, forgotten …

Whale: You're not a very tasty dish,
And you smell a trifle rotten.
Besides, you sit in the belly of a whale,
Whose rib cage you are breaking.
You sit in the belly of a humpback whale
And *you* are bellyaching!

Anna Livia Oysterface Steps Out

I scrub my back
and forth and back
with perfumed mud and oils.

I loosen my hair
and down it falls
in softly winding coils.

I redden my lips,
darken my eyes,
and, seated upon a pillow,
I weave a garland of meadow grass
with fallen leaves
of willow.

I fashion a necklace
of pebbles and cobbles,
with stones like the eyes of a cat.
I put on my gown,
odd clodhopper shoes,
and a pointy sugarloaf hat.

From my son, the postman,
I borrow a sack
and fill it with gifts for all.
Then shifting it back and forth
on my back,
I step out queenly and tall.

Passover

Tonight we eat unleavened bread
And males wear beanies on their head.

So who cares if we can't have challah?
'Tis the season to be jolla.

Hail the prophet who brought down The Law
From the mountain.
Hail Genesis, Exodus, Numbers (who's
countin'?).

Let sword and shield be broken;
Let persecution cease.
Hail the Festival of Freedom;
Speed the Passover of Peace.

We Three Queens of Orient Are

We three queens of Orient are
Bearing gifts we traverse afar.

What do we bring through wind and cold?
Myrrh, sweet frankincense, and gold.

And clothing and covers of infant size.
A bonnet to keep the sun from His eyes.
Diapers and ditties and old lullabies.
We bring them all from afar.

The Watched Pot

"You are watching me,"
said the steaming pot.

"So what?"
said the tick-tock clock.
"So what?"

"I'll tell you what,"
said the steaming pot.
"A watched pot never boils.
Never!"

"Tick-tock,"
mocked the clock.
"Did you say never?
You think you can go on
forever,
ever and ever,
just making steam?"

"I can,"
shrieked the pot.
"I'll scream, I'll scream."

"Watch out,"
said the clock.
"You'll blow your lid."

And the pot got boiling mad—and did!

Song of the River Lady

We feel as sad as the Liffey is long
for Mummy keeps singing
the same so sad song:

"Let the rain fall,
if it likes.
It's time for me to go.
But don't rush me,
for goodness sykes—
I likes to go real slow."

Here Comes Pretty Mummy

Here comes pretty Mummy
Giddy gaddy Mummy
Flopping on her elbows
Plopping on her tummy
Ducking under bridges
Dodging bits of bog
Swatting at the midges
Singing through the fog
Ah, bright sun merrying over the sea,
Bring back my mummy to me, back to me.

Yo!

Yo!
Here I come
Your darling mum
Zooming round the bay
Gig goggle of giggles
Hooray hooray
Gig goggle of giggles
Joy day!

For Humpy My Dumpy

For Humpy my dumpy,
who sits on high walls,
I carry a gluepot
for after his falls.
Unlike the king's horses
and all the king's men,
I can put Humpy
together again.
For Humpy my dumpy,
egg of my life,
gluepots of love

from Anna,
your wife.

By a Limpidy Stream

By a limpidy stream
I have a room.
I sweep it clean
with a limpidy broom.
I weave old dreams
on a limpidy loom.

If you come at twilight
and pass my room,
wave to me
through the welcoming gloom.

The Picnic

The old washerwoman was heard to complain,
"I hope for the picnic it just pours down rain,
for I can't find the pickles or gooseberry jam,
and I'm fed up with picnics, I am, yes I am."

The Washerwomen

Spread the wash on your side and I'll spread mine on mine.
It's so dismal damp today. I wish the sun would shine.

Me too, I feel all aches and pains, heavy as a stone.
I'm glad you're just across from me. At least I'm not alone.

The wind is rising. I feel cold.
Let's part and meet again.

You choose the place.
I'll choose the time.
Then you will have to make the rhyme.

Isabelle's Song

Bluebell,
scallop shell,
a lovely lass
named Isabelle
rides at night
on a carousel.
Up and down
and round she goes,
talking of naught
but tumty-tum-toes.

Gentlemen this and gentlemen that,
gentlemen medium, portly, and squat,
gentlemen short and gentlemen tall,
and one gent so small he's hardly at all.

Isabelle as Nuvoletta

Nuvoletta,
little cloud,
sang to her cloudy friends
aloud:

"Watch me go round
the sun,
watch me go round
the moon,
watch me turn into
a small gray puff
on a rainy afternoon.

"I rise with the sun
and fall with the rain,
falling and rising
all over again."

Is There One Who Understands Me?

Is there one who understands me?
I'm as lonely as the moon.
Let what happens happen.
Let it happen soon.

In a thousand years of days,
I did the best I could.
And in the whole big widey world,
no one understood.

Twenty-nine Girls

Twenty-nine girls
with fifty-eight feet
sat down where the Liffey flows.

Said all of the twenty-nine girls, "We know
what nobody else here knows:
that twenty-nine girls
with fifty-eight feet
have almost three hundred toes.

"We have precisely 2-9-0.
Let us count them one by one."
And so they did.
They counted them all and began all over for fun.

29 girls x 2 feet = 58 feet
58 feet x 5 toes = 290 toes

Cluck-Cluck

"Cluck-cluck, what luck
I found this letter-letter,"
said the hen.

"I found it in a muddy dump,
I can't remember when.
I wonder what this murky furky toodle
is about.

"My mother taught me how to cluck,
not read and find things out.
It's written on a biggish piece of paper,
stained with tea.

"Cluck-cluck, what luck
I found it, for it's clearly up to me
to deliver this good letter
from here to who knows where?

"It could be miles and miles away.
It could be over there."

Anna's Dream

"I had a curious dream," said Anna.
"I was a river flowing,
and all of my friends shouted,
'Annie, dear Annie,
where do you think you are going?'

"'I wish I knew,
but I haven't a clue,'
I said. 'But you'll see me soon:
in the chilly paw of a williwaw
or high in the eye of the moon.'"

God Punished the Moon

God punished the moon
by dimming her light
because she spoke ill of the sun.

Enfeebled and darkling
she fell through the night
releasing the stars one by one.